To the Living Memory of

LAMA NORLHA RINPOCHE

from whom I learned

the unity of the Cup and its contents

THE CUP

Other titles by Robert Kelly
published by McPherson & Company

A Transparent Tree
Cat Scratch Fever
Doctor of Silence
The Garden of Distances (with Brigitte Mahlknecht)
The Logic of the World
Queen of Terrors
Shadow Talk
Shame/Scham (with Birgit Kempker)
The Collected Stories
Unquell the Dawn Now (with Schuldt)

THE CUP

a pilgrimage

ROBERT KELLY

McPherson & Company

KINGSTON, NEW YORK

2021

Published by McPherson & Company
P.O. Box 1126 Kingston, NY 12402
WWW.MCPHERSONCO.COM
Book design by Bruce R. McPherson.
Printed on pH neutral paper.
Typeset in Truesdell.
First Edition

978-1-62054-045-9
1 3 5 7 9 10 8 6 4 2 2021 2022 2023 2024

LIBRARY OF CONGRESS CATALOGING-IN-PUBLICATION DATA

Names: Kelly, Robert, 1935- author.
Title: The cup : a pilgrimage / Robert Kelly.
Description: Kingston, New York : McPherson & Company, 2021.
Identifiers: LCCN 2021031307 | ISBN 9781620540459 (paperback)
Subjects: LCGFT: Poetry.
Classification: LCC PS3521.E4322 C87 2021 | DDC 811/.54--dc23
LC record available at https://lccn.loc.gov/2021031307

Manufactured in the United States of America.

Preface

With this poem I feel I'm paying my dues. My debt. From childhood on I have been caught up in the mystery and legend of the Holy Grail, so much so that when I was in graduate school I worked in medieval studies, concentrating on the British ramifications of the Arthurian stories, the Company of the Grail. When all the course work was done, I balked at the idea of the dissertation. Foolish as Parsifal, I drew back, said No, I am a poet, and left the degree unwon. I have never regretted that move, and lacking a PhD has not kept me from teaching joyously all over the place for sixty years mostly at Bard College, a place with its own enchantments. But I finally realize I do owe the Grail something, something at least as substantial as a poem. I tend to stare at things, a habit I learned from my father, one more indebtedness, and one day I sat watching a small bronze cup on the window ledge, a gift brought to me from the Near East…

THE CUP

1

John gave it to James,
dented bronze more tin than copper,
wrapped in a sweat-stained rag.
His sweat, John said. His?
James asked. His own, and traces
of his spittle on the rim.
—What am I to do with it?
John smiled at the question and said
Your whole life now is doing with it.
Did he say that? He made me
understand it.
No smile now.
Both men rapt in the sorrow of their loss.

2

Where is going anywhere?
To start with nothing and be everywhere?
Yaakov. Lame, lamed by an *ish*,
call it angel. Jacob. Jacobus. Jacomus.
James.
What is this in my name?
I stumble along, maimed by thought.
Yet I get there. Here.

3

What is this in my hands?
The cup he drank from
and made us drink too,
saying something about
drinking this was drinking
him, taking him inside.
Where no one could find him.
Maybe not even me.

4

John though had such quiet,
words came slowly
but when they came
they were like suddenly being naked,
knowing so much about yourself and everything.
You were young once, he said,
you understand.

5

James did. Understanding
means willingness.
I will take this cup and go
broadshouldered through
all the musics that must come,

the weather, the stone road
that leads to the sea.
Only the sea knows what happens then.

6

What a strange thing
a cup is.
It holds and it spills,
stands and falls,
quenches and surfeits,
offers libations to God
drinks with the devil.
Is there a devil?
By this point in history
only the cup knows.

7

Where shall I take it?

Let it take you.

He stared at the thing in his hands,
brought it to his lips,
whispered Where do you want to go?

Drink me, for I am empty
the cup whispered back,

and his mouth took on a tinny taste
and you will always be full.

But where do you go?

We, not me.

Where, then, do we go?

Don't speculate, read the evidence:
where everything goes.
Let the Sun remind you,
it all comes from the east,
the breast, it all
goes west, over the river,
over the sea —
go west as you can.

8

Strange thing cup is.
Hold to ear,
tap with fingernail
a sound like *think*
comes out, with overtones,
like a church bell,
later, later,
a decent church
is a cup offered on the ground.

9

Crater, *krater*, bowl,
drinking cup, the moon
is full of such churches

10

So James went West
as far as I can.
Went, goes, who knows
if he's still traveling,
all we have are his footsteps,
the shadow of a cup,
the sound it made once
when he poured it,
the taste in my mouth.

11

Don't leave anything out.
Boat by boat
he willed himself west

but leave all the stories out
fell to him along the way,
a cup is the opposite of a story,
a cup is in your hands,
a cup (lift it to your mouth,

slowly, you'll understand)
a cup says Nothing happens.
Just you and me.
Just you and me
quiet together, talking,
caring into each other.

12

In the antechamber of the sea
the women were discussing him.
He heard the rustle of their leafy gowns,
chlamyses and robes of state,
but couldn't understand their words.
He could tell they meant about him
by the way they kept looking,
laughed or smiled then looked away,
you can always tell
when they're talking
but seldom understand what they say.

13

At least he had gotten
far enough so he could hear them,
see them in sunlight
after all the Cypruses and Italies

and Sicilies and Spains
to be here at last,
the place from which there is nowhere to go.
He sat down on the sand
and set the cup with weary wonder
still tender practiced care
upright on a level rock
and let the sky fill it up with light
or whatever the cup would hold
of whatever the sky lets down.

14

There is always choosing
to be done.
Let the cup,
let the cup do it for you,
he taught it how to do that,
long ago, when it was,
just for an hour, just for a quick meal,
in *his* hand, bringing
whatever the wet earth had to offer
to *his* mouth wet
with *his* words.
The words fell in the cup and stayed.

15

The edge. He had come
to the edge of what he knew
as he looked out onto the Atlantic
as I am doing now
that it spoke the same language as the cup,
a little clearer than what those women sang,
and he caught a word from time to time,
words make sentences
and sentences make time.

16

James had learned from John
a word some Greek explained
later on his way through Kalavrita —
hypnopaideia, the Oldman in the tavern
sounded it like eep-no-pay-thee-a
so James kept waiting
for what he wasn't to be paid for
though he knew better.
The word meant education by dream
and we Jews have it too he knew,
Celestial Academy, Pumbedita Aloft
where the sages sit around with angels
and read the scrolls — awake,
we see them as clouds passing, staying.

17

So it was in dream
James did most of his learning,
John most of his teaching.

And one night he dared to ask:
But how did my brother get it,
why did he make such a fuss over it
and why do you?
John feared that now
he would have to tell the story,
he hated story, story is the opposite of glory,
glory happens all at once and always,
everything is now and no thing follows,
we are all together and we sing like birds!
he thought, but it was his job
to teach in dream
so he began.

18

As you know
as soon as he had his Bar Mitzvah
your brother set out east
to learn where the Sun is coming from
and what She learned along the way

and what She taught. Recall
that when he was born those Persian
wizards we hear so much about
had come by for a visit. So he wanted
to see where they came from too.
You know all of that, how far he went,
to where men wear pigtails and drink no milk,
he went all over and started back.
And then in an open market in Ladakh —
cold and high and dry he said, brrr —
he found this cup on a vegetable stall,
lying on its dented side among the cabbages;
it caught his eye, then took his hand,
felt strange and good, he asked what is this?
A cup from Kailash, she said, where Buddha swam.
Her eyes were amber, and she smiled.
I'll take it, your brother said, how much?
Take it with you, no money, no money.
you're not buying it — the cup is buying you.
Then she giggled just like a girl
though he knew she was far older than that.

19

But Kailash is a mountain, he knew, and said.
Yes, she answered, but at its base a holy lake,

the Wisdom Sea we say, there is a Queen of it.
Who knows? She may have drunk from it herself.
People will tell you all kinds of things —
just let the cup explain itself to you. Take it,
you'll be glad. I like your name, by the way,
it's like our word Yeshe, it means wisdom,
the knowing from which the world was made.

20

I don't much like talking
as I walk, so when I found myself
seated beside this woman
at breakfast, just coffee
and bread, after we'd walked
unspeaking a mile or two
before, I said to her
Why do you walk so far
so long? Is there a truth
at the end of that famous road,
or is it just (as we
existentialists suppose)
the truth of walking,
the truth of doing anything at all?

21

The pilgrim shifted on her bench
(we were outside the inn,
people nearby, embodying the norm)
she turned a little to look at me,
looked into my eyes and asked in turn:
Don't you know?
Women unnerve me with their directness,
I felt lost, muffled in subtleties
that really didn't matter.
I was silent, then said,
Honestly, I don't. I've met,
I've known, several people
(all women, strangely)
who took the pilgrim path,
this very one, maybe sat
on this same bench to drink
their Orangina or their kir,
depending, always depending,
I never asked them,
I was afraid of knowing,
afraid they'd make me
walk the same road too.

22

So to distract us both
I sang a little song,
soft as Reynaldo Hahn or Fauré:

I love to travel
I love to go
my favorite road
leads right here
to where I am
the longest road
leads me to me.

23

Halfway through my tune
she looked away,
another pilgrim
coming over the hill,
her heart went out to him,
left me sprawled
on the sands of my sad song.

24

She went on ahead of me
I watched her as I followed.
I won't go all the way,

I thought, why should I,
everything I look for is here,
wherever here is, wherever
it is I stand.
But I kept walking,
following one who seemed
to know the way.

25

In a quarter-mile or so
she stopped and turned round,
walked up to me.
You've had enough,
she said, angry.
Enough of what? I begged.
Enough of me —
it is wrong to watch me
from behind, me or anyone,
what we look like from behind
is a secret from ourselves
we hate to share with strangers.
You think you're watching
my shoulders and hips,
my gait, my style
but unknown to you
you are watching me,

a me that I can't ever see.
I don't mind if you stare
at me across the table
or across the room, I'll
stare right back or look away.
But this vigil you kept
on how I move
and how I am,
who I am,
angers me —
I could feel it
like a chill wind, turned
to find you. Here.
Now you walk ahead
or walk at my side.

26

We were between Ochoa and Azeri,
a blank stretch of sparse woodland
full of sky and stones.
James must have come this way
I thought out loud,
she said the book said so too,
I didn't ask what book,
I didn't want to read
I wanted, I want to be.

27

The woods are full of foxes
she explained, the town though
is clean and cheap — stay there and dream
but leave me out of your dreams,
go on alone. Every pilgrim is on
a road of her own, she intoned,
quoting another book I'll never read.

28

I was, unusual for me,
wise enough to shut up.
She went on ahead and I sat still,
by the fountain in a shabby public square,
the fountain had a saint on it
gushing water from a cup he held,
three stone-carved fish were by his feet
looking up as if to see
where the ocean of the world is coming from.

29

I can't help it now
I was born a Catholic
this round of time,
I can help a little

what I'll be next time.
So saints and crosses
have their way with me
still. Not the way
of credence or practice
but the way of feel.
As I now kneel before you,
love, I used to kneel
before a dead man on a tree
who taught me everything I know.

30

I met James along the way,
let me help you carry it.
It's not it, it's him.
And you already do.

31

Whenever I study the sea
(a verb that means my zeal
in doing it, not the sagesse
with which a scientist would bring)
whenever I study the sea
I understand why he came here,
why James knew, at least his legs
and body knew, where to bring the cup.

How hard it must have been —
for Jacob was lame, but knew the way.
And all these pilgrims take on themselves
the ardor and exhaustion of his passage
to get here. I swear it's not Compostela —
there are a thousand hidden shrines along
the ancient seacoasts of this little planet —
what a small planet to have such lives in it!

32

I used to wonder
why they said
my middle name was James
— Jacobus on the document.
I knew no Jameses
bar Jesse and Henry
whose several instincts
were remote from mine.
But then I learned, late,
who James's brother was.
But why am I bothering you
with chattering kid stuff like this?
I am a baby brother and I babble.

33

Because the water hisses
as it goes back out
sluicing through the pebbles
down at Church's Beach,
the sea roars in, the land
hushes it away it seems.
No information without static.
No music without mistakes.
And in great poetry mistakes
are the deepest meaning of the text —
like Kafka, Virgil said Burn my book.

34

So James had to listen to the sea —
that's what I'm trying to make clear.
That he did, and what he learned.
All times and all places
make sense of me
but by no means do all
of them call me by the name you know —
I am for everyone
and every other you reach
out to touch is a form of me —
I am the sacred Other of the world.
Honor me by cherishing all of them.

35

James wrote that down somewhere
but I can't find the book.
So let this be the end of the boring part —
back to the road where the story goes.
I mean the glory.

36

All right. We're there.
Here. The pilgrimage
of every day we talk
about is sheer consolation.
The real one is hard,
is far, hurts to get there
and you never get back.
How can you get back
from being where you are?

37

He sat me down at a bare table
and said sit there, I'll show it to you.
He went off into the shadows
so I sat. I admired
the intricate grain of the wood
of the tabletop, quiet shine

polished with kind use. Soon
he came back. I like the table I said
(I'm always talking)
the wood is beautiful,
I love wood. He looked at me, odd smile,
rueful, like the barber in *Shoah*,
and said Wood has many uses, remember,
many uses, and his eyes seemed to tear.

38

Anyhow he set it down before me,
the famous cup. Touch it, he said,
you can touch it with your hands,
hands are pure, or can be purified.
We don't need to wash
our hands to touch each other.
Just don't think it too much —
it's harder to purify the mind.
I reached out both hands and quietly,
reverently as I supposed, cupped the cup.
Nothing happened. Stop it, he said,
you're thinking, expecting, judging, waiting.
Nothing happens. It takes its time in you.

39

The fog is lifting
the land is coming back.
But from where James stood
there was no land to be seen,
nothing on horizon,
no island but me.
How far does this sea go
I asked out loud, and in my head
it said Two thousand years.

40

I put the cup down gently
she picked it up and wrapped it
in a dirty rag — Is that the cloth,
his sweat, his DNA?
Of course it is, she said,
what other cotton would burn so much?
and she touched the back of my wrist,
her fingertips were hot as new-baked bread.

41

I wish I knew the right thing to say
but I'm stymied by the wonders that I held
in my cold fingers such warmth of truth —

Stop that, James said, you're thinking again,
lyricking away instead of letting.
The woman beside you
seems to go a better way.

42

John had said. I was close
but you are blood,
so much of what he gave me
is in you too,
Now you have to find them,
let them surface,
let him speak.
And then John was gone,
left for his island — his Patmos,
a privilege (he explained)
because an island is all coast,
hardly any land,
almost like living as the sea.

43

I think I'm not the one
who started out.
I happened different along the way,
things keep making me up
and you do too I said to her

when we happened to sit together
at a restaurant in Los Robles —
which I think means oak trees —
she was leaving as I was coming in,
we sat together, I did all the talking.
What does happen in you,
she said. You make me go,
if you were not on the road
I'd still be at home on my own island,
it would be years ago
and I would still be me,
would be sitting somewhere
under an ancient apple tree
writing in my notebook,
reading the news, watching
the island move among the ferns.

Fern seed is almost invisible
she said, got up and left the place.
I had to walk the next few miles
working at what she meant by that.
I never did — can you?

44

For most of them, the cup
was an excuse

to fight and romance and conquer,
for some though a sign of union,
community, collegium, band.
A sign to seek. A mystery
that only worked when left unsolved.

But all the while the real cup was doing,
speaking its own texts into our hearts,
so many minds, even those who didn't know
that they were hearing, hearing it —
they thought they were just thinking.

45

James had come out to meet us
on the town's edge,
he liked edges, he explained,
you can see the center best from there.
He stood before the few of us
who had come this far,
and in a lecturing tone began:

Without Dharma
live at loose ends,
no foundation.
Dharma means *firm*
in your language,
means getting it right,

Dharma means help
everybody, hurt no one,
Dharma means knowing the score.

I woke then
from the dream of him
waiting for us at the end of the camino.
I was at home, where I always am,
some sleep, some wake.
I looked up his word,
Sanskrit I read in my sleep.
Not everything that speaks
in dream is true, I thought.
And it said: this is no dream.

46

I feel guilty, awkward,
I sit here holding the cup
not thinking much,
not feeling anything special,
not asking big questions.
What am I doing wrong?
The cup is not about thinking
he said, not about feeling.
Sit there, shut up,
like a wise child,

nothing to wait for,
everything is now.

47

He handed me a cloth -bound book
stamped in gold
THE NEWER TESTAMENT.
But all the pages are blank.
He smiled as if to say
It's up to you.
I tried
to wake up then
but sleep has soft fragrant
arms that hold me close.

48

Can I mark the meaning?
Cup. Can I walk the water?

Cup. Can I fly even? Maybe,
ask your pastor, the indoor
shepherd who lives in your heart—
in the old garage by the mitral valve.

You lost me.
I will never lose you.

49

Say each word twice,
once for your father,
once for your mother —
you are the space between

50

We talked that way all day long
I seldom understood but seldom said so,
fearing the calculus of his explanation.

51

So, young man, he began one day
as we were seated on a bench
above the ocean, a pelican or some
such thing perched beside us.
How can you call me young,
with all my decades on me?
All living men are young
compared to me, two
thousand summers have I lived.
Only certain women are my elders —
and you're still too young
to learn about them.

52

The sun is what boys used to call
a hot tomato. The moon
is a shy young man,
seldom shows his full self —
is that the truth they've all been hiding?
Is that what I should take home from this tryst?

53

Who is today after all
but the star I kissed last night?

But what does that *mean*?
I wanted, and he didn't know.

But I know what you mean:
he said, a license to let time

pass fast and a wall clock
that tells no scary stories

and a waiter sets a silk rose on your table
a slice of lemon, a slice of fried fish.

54

But I still didn't know
Is it a judgment on me,
this ignorance? Silence,
slave! he roared, there is
a sea gull perching on your roof.

55

The road was so long.
So long we used to say
to mean good-bye. Now
we have come to the place
to which all the departures
bent their way, all the good-byes
came home. The maps
just call it the sea: *Mare*
Atlanticum, sea of Atlantis,
we think of it as where we ourselves
came from, or else the way
we came to the new world
we thought it was. But this
old coast is the newest world of all.
James came here and set the cup down.

56

Rather than the window,
there was only one, chose
the door, stood by it to wait
for it to open, she stared
at the wood, felt safe
in its opacity. The grain
of wood is many rivers
she thought, rivers of Eden
countless, flowing through
all our lives, carrying what
information, she wondered,
eels, rafts, pale Melusina?
The door was silent.

57

He had never said so
in so many words
but she felt he had promised
to come join her there —
several sentences left unsaid
scraps of phrases passing
about the sea coast, the waves'
song, or quoting that Greek poem
about *the fishy depths of sea*

beyond Byzantium. Well,
she was far beyond The City
now, other end of the known world.
And where was he? Why
did he keep her waiting? And another
question, a little frightening,
why did it feel so good to wait?

58

I looked up from Miriam's memoir,
closed the book.
What if every woman I ever knew
had come this way?
Had they all stood at the door,
dreaming what the old oak grain
instructed, all waited for him,
and was everyone I have ever been
just a callow imposter,
well-meaning fake,
a stand-in for the real?
I felt I should never knock on a door again.

59

Outside, the pilgrims
were clamoring for Mass.
By no means all of them

Catholics, but they knew
what was supposed to happen,
maybe no magic in the Mass,
the magic came in saying it,
hoping it, dreaming through it.
And they hoped it would be Latin
which is easier to dream through.

60

I didn't spot her in the crowd.
I'm getting tired of relationships
close or fraught, leave them alone,
leave me alone. I didn't mean it
and I was scared for a moment
that they had heard me, The Powers,
I take it back. I take it back.

61

To be precise, doctor, I was tired
of letting my experience of daily reality
be tethered to constant acts
of triangulation between her and me,
where is she now, what does she mean,
where did she go, what does she know,
who is she with and what does she say,
why do I watch her, why do I care,

why do I steadily trail behind
when I could rightly, richly,
stride on ahead, get there before her
not need anyone else? Then the doctor
who lives in my head, I call him Doctor
Hypothalamus (or hippo, sometimes,
Horsehead) stood up and answered me
and I recognized the voice as John's.

62

Because she knows
where the cup lives.
And you do not.
Because she cares
enough to spend her life
in traveling towards it
step by step.
And you do not.
You barely know enough
to follow her
and all like her,
yet dare to grumble
and growl along the way,
as if you expected
her and all like her
to turn back to you,

abandoning their quest —
do you think that you
yourself are the cup?
Only one man ever
is the cup, and he himself
is waiting for her at the end.
And into him all lives will pour
and be renewed.
Go, follow her
gladly, or stay home
and pretend to dream.

63

Of course I knew all that,
wanted to hear him say it.

I have been here since the beginning.
We all have. We know
this whole story in our bones.
All any song does is just remind.

64

An old man appeared from time to time
in the sanctuary to answer tourist questions.
Not clear if he's a priest, wears a surplice
over a black cassock but who knows,

she thought. Asked him: Is the cup we see
the actual original or a replica? Unsmiling,
he spoke gently: Everything is a replica.
This is what you call the original, but even
the original is a replica. Do you understand?
Do you mean that things are copies
of Platonic forms? Sorry to say, that man
never thought to come here, years later,
when he was reborn. Do you believe
in reincarnation? — she was surprised.
But he had turned away to the next pilgrim.

65

She told me all about it later
when she consented to take tea with me
at the Hotel St. James *con pies cojados*,
with wet feet, a curious name, maybe
he still is standing in the surf, maybe
we all are, eyes blurred with tears.
Get to the point, she said, what are you after
coming all this way, you don't even believe
in all this stuff, are you just following me?
And why would I do that? I had the wit to say.
Then she was silent and we both were sad.

66

I felt guilty for having silenced us
so I told the truth: You knew the way.
I followed you because you knew the way.
Most of the pilgrims stopped at Compostela
but you went on, all these miles more,
and I followed, I could tell you were
someone who knew something, even if
maybe you didn't know you knew,
but I could see that you knew the way.
Here, to this shambles of a chapel,
old altar, an old cup on it, dust everywhere
and yet you knew. You knew the way —
to the sea, the water where he stood,
where he washed the cup at last in water
older than anything he knew. You knew
the way. You led me, and now you know.
Thank you for being here before me, for me.

67

In an old house by another sea
(or are they all the same)
I found a wooden cup that looked
just like the one I think I saw
the Galician coast, only mine was wood,

and in the bowl of it a small insect
had come long ago to die
and in my hand I held its sepulcher.

68

Something's always
getting in the way of truth.
Sometimes I think reality
and truth are opposites
or even enemies. Sometimes
I look at the waves coming in
and know they wash away
each time everything I know
so all I'm left with is beholding
this water, this inward,
this outward flow, this going away.

69

Sigh. And go back
to the chapel
empty now, the cup
back in its tabernacle
I suppose they call it.
I love words. Why not?
They lie quiet in the mind
like old lovers, then all

at once they speak, call
even, so that you rouse
and look up, look away from the sea.

70

On a creaking pew
I found a note:
If you're looking for me
I've gone to the Wet Feet.
I was boy enough to be glad
of getting a note from her,
grammarian enough
to wonder where she'd be
if I weren't looking for her.
So I saddled my doubts
and made my way to the hotel.

71

James spoke to a lapwing
that landed at his feet.
O strange friend bird, he said,
please take for me a message
to my friend John, he lives
on an island far east of here —
can you do that? The bird
looked up and shook its head

but said, No, but I know
a swift who can — what saying?
Tell him that I have found the sea
and washed the cup and set it down
in a safe and honorable place.
The bird said He knows all that
already. And flew away.

72

There is no love
to be made between us
she said as we finished our tea.
An odd way of putting it
I thought, but only said
I had no hopes in that direction.
And that too sounded odd to me.

73

So James began to teach
and preach and went on meditating.
The shape of his prayers grew strange,
his brother seemed to have drained
the old words of their sense
and filled them with new excitement,
each blessing a revelation,
and every Thou and Thee a mystery —

to whom do we pray?
Or is praying aimed at anyone at all?
Is it the music of the mind
yearning for the listener of the world?

74

Should I not learn
what my prayer means
before I teach another
to say prayers?

Should I know the truth
entirely before
I open my mouth to proclaim
what I only hope is so?

Now brush these doubts aside
and mount the pulpit.
Their ears are waiting, maybe
their heart-minds too.

The only truth you hold
is what they make real
in themselves
from what you say.

75

Polo menos bícame
I said as we stood up
about to leave the table,
about to leave each other.
You looked that up, she said,
and no, there are no kisses
needed in our brief tryst.
I've given you all you need.

76

And that was the end of my meeting
with Saint Somebody of the Cup.
She went out quickly, and when I tried
to pay our bill the waiter said
The lady paid already, and he looked
as if something were my fault.
As it so often is. I did not see her more.

77

I stayed the night though
so next morning I could go
visit the ruined chapel again
before I too left this place.
And when I got there, sunlight

breathing through sea-fog,
the door was open and that old
priest-like character she'd seen
was standing in the doorway
arms half-spread in cautious welcome.
I meant to be polite and circumspect
but burst out with Where is it?

78

La cunca do seu irmán
that's what I'm looking for.
I've tried everything else
in this fucking world
and nothing helps. I suffer
from a nameless plague,
a psychic leprosy, I want
his brother's cup, I've come
all this way to get it, pretended
to be after a story or a woman
but it was always only this,
this thing I don't know, thing
I think I've seen, thing from which
I need to drink. His blood
or mine. Give it to me.

79

I can only give you
what you have already
but that is a princely gift,
you know so little
of what you are,
what is yours,
or even why you came
all this way, unknowing,
unthinking, but moving,
to touch my brother's cup.

80

Your brother? I was amazed
but he: Hush, who else
would you expect to interview
in the special dream or vision
you can have only in this place?
Why else come here? Place
has meaning. Place remembers.
Place understands what happens
where it is. Place can speak
and this place does, and you right
now are hearing what it had of me,
Yakov the West Wanderer, the brother.
Come, I'll let you touch the cup.

81

Streets are made of dream.
And streets, straights, stresses
that's what they are. Our fancy words,
road, highway, boulevard, camino,
don't believe them for a moment.
They are streets. And all the streets
in the world lead right here. I mean
where you are. Where I was
when the dream broke and I was left
sitting on a boulder watching the sea.
Trying to learn the dialects of ocean,
this Galician coast, my own Massachusetts,
Molokai, Donegal, Venezia, Whitby, Oregon.
I understand most of what I hear
but have no words of it to answer back.

82

Sometimes I look
at my little
wooden chalice
on a table in the cellar.
Sometimes I think
I see a dove,
white one, not the grey

murmurers of this coast,
hovering over it,
or just a grey dove
after all with a scrap
of white bread in its beak
as if to dip it
in the hollow mystery of cup.
The little chalice
lets me be
a priest of it and say its Mass
in my devious Latin —
and this too is his body
by which we are all sustained.

83

So only after she was gone
did I let myself acknowledge
how much I had wanted, I wanted,
to be with her. Was it her knowing
mind I craved, or her woman-ness
that I am programmed to desire?
I did not know. Not even know
if there's any real difference between
mind and body. We think
with our feet, pilgrims all our days.

84

And James beheld all this
as he has for so many years,
the stumbling confusions
of the pilgrims, these would-be
conquistadors of spirit.
And James wrote down as usual
the vital facts in his ledger, a book
made out of rock, deep embedded
in the foreshore, his skinny pen lines
leave little veins of meaning in the stone.
The ocean reads such things
and duly carries them to their intended.

85

So John on his far island heard
this one more saddish story.
Go after him and change his mind!
he cried into the east wind
so James heard half an hour later.
Up he rises and hovers over
the trudging not-quite-lover
going back to the womanless hotel.
James took the form of a child,
a dusky little girl who carried

two paper cups of something
careful not to spill them. And one
she sipped from and one she gave
to our American friend. Startled
he sipped it too, and all his sorrow
fell away. I am what I am, no more
and no less, I will go on to the end
he thought, not even caring what
the end might be. Gracias, muchas
gracias he said, but the child was gone
when he looked up from the cup.

86

But I have said all this before.
The swan is a pigeon
caught in the subway tunnel.
Maybe he just wants to be there,
amused by the signal lights,
the red, the green, the blue
that used to charm me
just after the Nevins station.
Please don't bother to remember.
Nothing is worth leaving this moment for.
As I said, as I have said before.

87

The peaceful disorder of pilgrims
trying to understand
where they're going and why.
Going (in German it can mean walking)
(andante, slowly, afoot), going
is so provisional, can stop
anywhere at all and there you are.
Some pilgrims sing hymns as they go,
some say the rosary, their fingers
going endlessly around a wreath
of roses the Crusaders brought back
from the Sufis, who got it from
North Indian Hindus and Buddhists
Om mani peme hum. The pilgrims use
other words, I think they mean the same.
Lead me to the truth and let me be it, O
Woman who smuggled truth into the world.

88

So much for love
he thought
and smiled at the sparrows
dust-bathing on the path.
Am I cleansed

by my defilements? Don't
be so fond of paradox,
remember what it did to Socrates.
He tried to puzzle that out as he walked.

89

As he passed
that first time
through Galicia
he had the hospitality
of a pagan holy site
with pleasant
druidy priests.
He tamed them
and taught them,
left them happy,
gave the site
new meaning and new
breath, and it
breathes still. But he
kept going till he reached
the sea. The cup
led him right down to the surf,
he rinsed it out, the cup
and the sea drank each other
and James filled the cup,

drank it down, shook
the last drops and let the cup
fill with meaningful emptiness.
That is the whole story.
That is why it cures or heals
or does whatever you think it does.
That is the whole story.
All the rest
is colors and smells
seashells and weavings
swords and princesses,
guesses and dreams
and roads, so many roads.

Now here it is.

90

Who spoke?
who heard?
Something happened,
someone's lips
were full of taste.
Full of praise.

91

Then from a hidden aumbry in the wall
he took the battered cup
and raised it to my lips
the way Anglicans used to do
and I drank what was in it.
All I could taste was air
but I did taste that
and air is all we really need to live.
This air tasted of the ocean —
You understand, he said, as he put it back,
the cup has changed the sea.

15 June – 1 July 2019
Cuttyhunk Island